MANCHESTER TERRIER

BACK
Slight arch, falling slightly
to the tail set

TAIL
Moderately
short

THIGH
Muscular

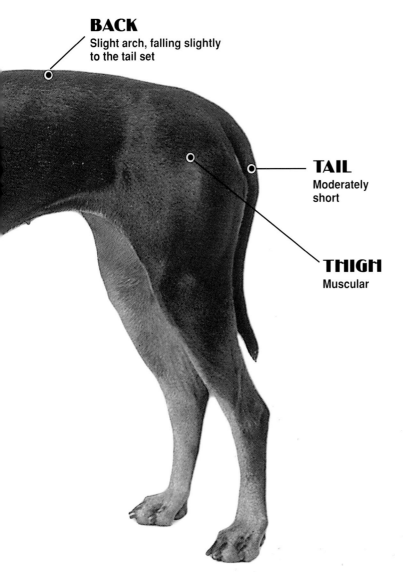

Title page: Manchester Terrier photographed by Gregory Scott McLaine

Photographers: Rich Bergman, Isabelle Francais, Gregory Scott McLaine, Robert Pearcy, Kitten Rodwell, and Phil Shane

---

Dedication

In Memory of Rosewood Sir Sydney, a special friend.

Distributed in the UNITED STATES to the Pet Trade by T.F.H. Publications, Inc., 1 TFH Plaza, Neptune City, NJ 07753; on the Internet at www.tfh.com; in CANADA by Rolf C. Hagen Inc., 3225 Sartelon St., Montreal, Quebec H4R 1E8; Pet Trade by H & L Pet Supplies Inc., 27 Kingston Crescent, Kitchener, Ontario N2B 2T6; in ENGLAND by T.F.H. Publications, PO Box 74, Havant PO9 5TT; in AUSTRALIA AND THE SOUTH PACIFIC by T.F.H. (Australia), Pty. Ltd., Box 149, Brookvale 2100 N.S.W., Australia; in NEW ZEALAND by Brooklands Aquarium Ltd., 5 McGiven Drive, New Plymouth, RD1 New Zealand; in SOUTH AFRICA by Rolf C. Hagen S.A. (PTY.) LTD., P.O. Box 201199, Durban North 4016, South Africa; in JAPAN by T.F.H. Publications, Japan—Jiro Tsuda, 10-12-3 Ohjidai, Sakura, Chiba 285, Japan. Published by T.F.H. Publications, Inc.

MANUFACTURED IN THE
UNITED STATES OF AMERICA
BY T.F.H. PUBLICATIONS, INC.

MANCHESTER TERRIER

A COMPLETE AND RELIABLE HANDBOOK

Phil Shane

RX-105

CONTENTS

HISTORY OF THE MANCHESTER TERRIER

The Manchester Terrier has the singular enviable distinction of being the oldest of all the recognized Terrier breeds. As early on as 1500, we see mention of a Manchester terrier-type dog made by Dr. Caius in *De Banibus Britannicis*, the first written documentation of dogs. The British artwork of the mid-1700s clearly depicts a dog called the Black and Tan or Rat Terrier as closely resembling today's Manchester Terrier. However, by the year 1800, Sydenham Edwards had published *Cynographia Britannica*, that includes an entry on the Manchester Terrier, as well as illustrations including all the fancier's touches.

The Manchester Terrier has an illustrious history dating back to the early 14th century, predating all other terrier breeds.

7

The actual history of the Manchester Terrier lies somewhere in an overly populated province of medieval England. At this time in history, dogs were not necessarily kept as pets by the common folk but as working members of a household who earned their keep. The Black and Tan Terrier, as he was then called, was well known for his accomplishments as a vermin extinguisher. These dogs were extremely responsive and revered for their lightning-fast reflexes. One story recounts a tale of almost certainly exaggerated proportions in which a dog is said to have killed over 100 rats within minutes. These legends soon spread throughout the surrounding area and the dogs were commissioned to work in other areas suffering from gross rat infestation.

At some point in the early 1800s, Manchester, England became known as the epicenter for the newly popular sports of rat killing and rabbit coursing. A fancier by the name of John Hulme decided there should be one dog that excelled at both. In an effort to produce this dog, he mated a Whippet bitch with a dark-brown, rat-killing dog. The resulting offspring

The Manchester Terrier gained recognition because of his legendary ability to hunt vermin.

exhibited the roached back of the Whippet, seldom found in other terrier breeds. The dogs proved useful, and eventually other fanciers began to breed them, thus beginning the advent of the Manchester Terrier.

Eventually, the dog gained recognition with the masses and he came to be included in the ever-popular sport of fox hunting, hence moving up the social ladder. The Manchester was the perfect companion for the men of the day, as opposed to the frilly lap dogs that the ladies were currently fancying and became known as the "gentleman's dog." He can be seen depicted as a small blackish dog in many of the old European portraits of the century.

It is not known how or why this new terrier came to be known as the Manchester because similar dogs existed throughout England. However, by 1860, the city for which the dog had been named had become a breed center.

Besides the Whippet, the Greyhound and the Italian Greyhound have also been mentioned as progenitors of the new Manchester breed. No one can say for sure which was the most influential, but they are generally all considered partners in the creation of the Manchester Terrier. There has been further suspicion that the Dachshund is also a relative of the Manchester Terrier, and although at first glance this relationship may seem unlikely, keep in mind that the Dachshunds of yesteryear were not the exaggerated, long, stubby-legged animals of today.

The Manchester Terrier's heritage lies in Manchester, England, in a once overly populated province of the same name.

THE TOY DEVELOPS

Documentation of the Toy Manchester's development is admittedly sketchy and therefore, little is known concerning the approximate date that the Toy first appeared. It is known that breeding the Toy was first a matter of chance, and only later when a demand was realized did the selection begin to play a role. Basically, what happened at first was that two normal-sized Manchesters would produce a litter of mainly normal-sized offspring. The so-called "runt" would attract tremendous attention and create a demand for more like him. Naturally, breeders were encouraged to produce more smaller-sized puppies. Unfortunately, along with this trend came extensive inbreeding because of the limited number of toy-sized dogs to breed from. In Victorian times, size diminished so alarmingly that the Toy Manchester weighed in at about two and one-half pounds and couldn't be considered anything but delicate. Soon, breeders came to realize the disadvantages and aimed for and finally bred a more normal Toy weight, along with a dog who exhibited the desired feist and attitude.

The early development of the Toy Manchester Terrier happened by chance—Toys were merely the smallest members of a litter.

The American Kennel Club recognized the Manchester Terrier as a breed in 1926.

THE MANCHESTER TERRIER'S ARRIVAL IN THE UNITED STATES

The first Manchester Terrier probably arrived in the United States around 1883. At first, the dog served the same purpose that he had in England. He could be found in residence at many barns, using his talent for rodent control.

It is not until 1923, with the formation of the Manchester Terrier Club of America, that we see any interest in the sport and breeding of Manchesters. Up until this time, there had been some confusion about what the breed was to be called. Some were referring to the dog as Black and Tan, others as the Rat Terrier. With the formation of the parent club, the name Manchester Terrier was brought to the fore and there it remained.

The breed standard was written and proposed by the parent club in about 1923 and the American Kennel Club recognized the breed around 1926. Until

1959, the Toy was regarded as a separate breed, though even today the two varieties are shown separately: the Toy Manchester in the Toy Group and the Standard in the Terrier Group.

Unfortunately, there has been a steady decline in the popularity and registration of the Manchester Terrier in recent years. Some feel that the drop-off is not so recent and actually harks back to the time when the anti-cropping edict was passed in England. At that time, it is said that many fanciers left the breed in frustration after not being able to produce quality dogs with naturally erect ears. It was left up to a few staunch devotees to keep the breed alive. Whatever the reason for the Manchester Terrier's lack of popularity, there are only approximately 500 dogs, both Standard and Toy, registered with the American Kennel Club today.

Although the breed standard for the Manchester Terrier and the Toy Manchester Terrier has always been the same, they were considered separate breeds up until 1959.

DESCRIPTION OF THE MANCHESTER TERRIER

The Toy Manchester Terrier is an exact replica of the Standard Manchester Terrier in miniature.

Toward the end of the Middle Ages, circa the late 1400s, a breed of sleek alert terrier emerged out of the crowded streets of Manchester, England. Known for their prowess as rat hunters, these Manchester Terriers, as they later became known, were much sought after in a land grown used to varmint infestation.

DESCRIPTION

As courageous and tough as he is feisty and affectionate, the Manchester Terrier makes a loyal, eager-to-please companion that can now be found participating in various aspects of life. Today he is as likely to be a competitor in the show ring exhibiting his regal carriage in cities throughout the world as he is to be a happy family member, intent on a wild game of chase with the children.

The Toy Manchester is merely a miniature version of the Manchester Terrier, a product of the selective breeding of the small offspring of Standard Manchester Terriers. In England, the breed is called the English Toy Terrier (Black and Tan). These days, the Toy commands special popularity because of his compact size. In this modern age of urban living, the Manchester is unmatched in his ability to adapt to any living circumstance, from cavernous mansion to small apartment. This loyal and courageous animal with the surprisingly strong bark makes a wonderful companion as well as watchdog.

Opposite: The loving and happy disposition of the Manchester Terrier makes him a welcome addition to most families.

The Manchester Terrier is a versatile animal—the perfect canine companion as well as a skilled hunter.

DESCRIPTION

Wherever he is known, he is adored for his charm and sensitivity. Extremely expressive and inquisitive, Manchesters know their owners as well as they know themselves. In stature and substance, he is very much a gentleman's dog, ready to meet any challenge with a spirit as great as he is small. However, one will never find an animal better suited to the parlors of discriminating homemakers. Well mannered in demeanor and of fastidiously clean comport, the Manchester Terrier is truly an asset to the most discerning companion.

APPEARANCE

The Toy Manchester Terrier is nearly a carbon copy of his slightly larger counterpart, the Standard Manchester Terrier. There is a well-bred look about both dogs and a sleekness that is rarely found in other breeds. Do not be fooled by the Toy's diminutive appearance; there is nothing fragile about this little dynamo. The Manchester has a long clean head, a sharp intelligent expression, and a glossy short black

The Manchester Terrier has a number of unique qualities that make him a versatile and amiable breed.

coat with rich mahogany tan markings on the face, legs, and chest. The length and color of the coat create a distinctive contrasting pattern, so fleas can be spotted immediately. They also have a well-proportioned, tapered, whip-like tail that remains uncropped and in earlier ages, served as a fifth leg for pivotal purposes during hunting.

The Manchester is an extremely clean breed that will not require much grooming except for the occasional bath. They do not shed much during the warmer summer months. He is well proportioned and has very nice lines. Among the leggier of the terrier breeds, he is known for his swiftness afoot and his graceful movement. The Toy Manchester weighs 12 pounds or under, as opposed to the Standard, who weighs up to 22 pounds. They have an average life span of up to 15 years.

Other than size, the greatest difference between the Toy and the Standard Manchester Terrier concerns the ears. The ears of the Standard Manchester may be carried erect or button; if they are cropped, they are long and carried straight up. However, the

According to the breed standard, the Standard Manchester Terrier's ears may be cropped or button.

Toy variety is automatically faulted if any ear cropping occurs. The Toy Manchester Terriers ears must be carried erect naturally without a sideways flare and are sometimes referred to as "candle flame" in appearance.

The Manchester Terrier's expression should reflect his alert and intelligent nature.

The eyes of a Manchester Terrier should be very dark, perhaps even bordering on black. The Manchester Terrier of today is slightly different in appearance than the black and tans of yesteryear. He exhibits that true Manchester type: flat skull, triangular eyes, accented cheekbones, and a sleek, dark, black coat with clearly delineated markings.

TEMPERAMENT AND PERSONALITY

The temperament of a Manchester Terrier is rather unique. The Manchester surely considers himself a regal being, both in carriage and temperament. He is known to carry his head high and is lauded for his superior coordination. An extremely cunning and intelligent dog, it is impossible to ignore his sparkling personality and insatiable eagerness to learn. The usual words used to describe various terrier breeds, such as stoic and dour, certainly do not apply to the Manchester.

The Manchester's sense of smell and excellent hearing are legendary, allowing for a keen sense of awareness that makes him especially alert. This will serve you well when relying on your Manchester as a watchdog, as he will surely warn you when someone is approaching. Another of the Manchester's interesting attributes is this little fellow's amazing agility. Surely a holdover from the past when the little dog could chase down and kill hundreds of rats in a single hour, the Manchester Terrier excels in agility trials of today. Not only can the Manchester maneuver, he is also renowned for his ability to jump and climb, as well as for his remarkable reflexes. Unbelievable as it may seem, these tiny creatures can easily jump up to three to four times their height. They have been known to climb fences in excess of six feet in height and react within seconds to any new stimuli. Despite their small

The long legs and sleek lines of the Manchester have earned him a reputation for swift and graceful movement.

stature, the Toy Manchester is surely an athletic dog, up to the challenge of living life to its fullest. For the most part, this is no stereotypical toy breed that will be content merely sitting upon your lap.

Both varieties of Manchester require plenty of outdoor activity and attention. They love to go on lengthy walks during the warm summer months. However, do not be foolish and attempt this on very cold days or in inclement weather. Because of the Manchester's short coat, the breed feels the cold intensely and abhors the rain. I assure you that on bad weather days you will have to practically drag the dog outdoors to attend to his needs. On the up side, the Manchester is an avid sunbather and enjoys quick dips in the kiddie pool or a large puddle to cool off. Keep in mind, however, that the Manchester Terrier should never be considered an outside dog.

Although their vision is generally unremarkable as far as dogs are concerned, it is important to remember that as a breed, their eyes do not adjust well to sudden darkness. One should consider his vision similar to that of humans. Much like us, it will take the Manchester several minutes to adjust to a dimly lit room or a dark evening outdoors.

Your Manchester Terrier will want to be involved in everything you do—even filling up the bird bath.

Opposite: The Manchester Terrier's fun-loving disposition makes him the perfect playmate for gentle children.

DESCRIPTION

Intensely sensitive, the Manchester is the epitome of human's best friend. At times, the dog seems uncannily tuned into the feeling of his human counterparts and, on the other hand, amazingly aware of his own emotional reactions. When scolding is necessary, the Manchester is likely to pout for hours and attempt reconciliation as often as permitted. Once forgiven, he is jubilant and quick to forget the incident that brought about his sorrowful state in the first place.

Along with the intelligent nature of the Manchester comes an overwhelming curiosity that leads many to regard him as downright nosy. Worth mentioning again is the breed's adaptability to any and all living conditions. The Manchester Terrier requires very little to make him a happy, well-adjusted member of the family. They are always ready to play with just about anything that can be found around the house and are especially fond of squeaky toys. Although I have found that they are very fond of playing with a pair of socks tied into a knot, there are dozens of safer, better chewing devices at your local petshop. Consider introducing a Nylafloss® from Nylabone® or perhaps an edible treat such as a RoarHide™ or Carrot Bone™.

I would not necessarily consider the Manchester to be particularly well suited to life with small children. Because of the dog's small size, children have the advantage over this intelligent and sensitive creature, and the quick grabbing movements of children will be most unappreciated.

Whether male or female, the Manchester puppy you choose will make an equally loving and devoted companion.

Carrots are rich in fiber, carbohydrates, and Vitamin A. The Carrot Bone™ by Nylabone® is a durable chew containing no plastics or artificial ingredients and it can be served as-is, in a bone-hard form, or microwaved to a biscuit consistency.

Although the Manchester Terrier will very rarely bite when upset, they will become more standoffish and unwilling to approach even the most innocuous looking stranger. However, once both parties have been properly introduced and supervised, the Manchester will be most solicitous toward children.

Finally, it is important to remember that along with this unique terrier's intelligence comes a strong-willed personality. It is imperative that through bonding and proper training you establish yourself as the pack leader. The Manchester Terrier is always better off with something to occupy his quick mind, and he takes immeasurable pride in his accomplishments. Once a command or trick is taught, he will never forget it, and you may be surprised during lessons at how much he already knows.

There is no telling what life has in store for the Manchester Terrier puppy you choose—he may be a champion or companion—but he'll definitely be your best friend!

STANDARD OF THE MANCHESTER TERRIER

A standard is generally defined as something established by authority as a rule or example. This is precisely what the official standard for the Manchester Terrier accomplishes. It is a written description of the ideal Manchester Terrier and is the yardstick by which breeders and judges measure a particular dog against the ideal. The following standard is the approved standard of the American Kennel Club, the

The overall appearance of a Manchester Terrier should reflect power, endurance, agility, and animation.

country's largest dog registry, and the principal governing body for the dog sport in the United States. The standard is first proposed by the particular breed's parent club and then accepted by the AKC. The standard may undergo minor changes from time to time as the parent club dictates. Studying the breed standard will help any breed enthusiast become familiar with the more intricate details of a dog's ideal physique and character. Whether you are interested in breeding, showing, or simply enjoying your dog, the standard should be required reading for any breed fancier.

Although small, the Manchester Terrier is a well-balanced and compact dog.

OFFICIAL STANDARD OF THE MANCHESTER TERRIER

General Appearance—A small, black, short-coated dog with distinctive rich mahogany markings and a taper style tail. In structure the Manchester presents a sleek, sturdy, yet elegant look, and has a wedge-shaped, long and clean head with a keen, bright, alert expression. The smooth, compact, muscular body expresses great power and agility, enabling the Manchester to kill vermin and course small game.

Except for size and ear options, there are no differences between the Standard and Toy varieties of the Manchester Terrier. The Toy is a diminutive version of the Standard variety.

Size, Proportion, Substance—The *Toy variety* shall not exceed 12 pounds. It is suggested that clubs consider dividing the American-bred and Open classes by weight as follows: 7 pounds and under, over 7 pounds and not exceeding 12 pounds.

The *Standard variety* shall be over 12 pounds and not exceeding 22 pounds. Dogs weighing over 22 pounds shall be disqualified. It is suggested that clubs consider dividing the American-bred and Open classes by weight as follows: over 12 pounds and not exceeding 16 pounds and not exceeding 22 pounds.

The Manchester Terrier, overall, is slightly longer than tall. The height, measured vertically from the ground to the highest point of the withers, is slightly less than the length, measured horizontally from the point of the shoulders to the rear projection of the upper thigh.

The sturdy Manchester Terrier should be slightly longer than he is tall.

The bone and muscle of the Manchester Terrier is of sufficient mass to ensure agility and endurance.

Head—The Manchester Terrier has a keen and alert *expression.*

The nearly black, almond shaped *eyes* are small, bright, and sparkling. They are set moderately close together, slanting upwards on the outside. The eyes neither protrude nor sink in the skull. Pigmentation must be black.

Correct *ears* for the *Standard variety* are either the naturally erect ear, the cropped ear, or the button ear. No preference is given to any of the ear types. The naturally erect ear, and the button ear, should be wider at the base tapering to pointed tips, and carried well up on the skull. Wide, flaring, blunt tipped, or "bell" ears are a serious fault. Cropped ears should be long, pointed and carried erect.

The Standard Manchester Terrier can weigh anywhere from 12 to 22 pounds.

The only correct **ear** for the *Toy variety* is the naturally erect ear. They should be wider at the base tapering to pointed tips, and carried well up on the skull. Wide, flaring, blunt tipped, or "bell" ears are a serious fault. Cropped, or cut ears are a disqualification in the Toy variety.

The **head** is long, narrow, tight skinned, and almost flat with a slight indentation up the forehead. It resembles a blunted wedge in frontal and profile views. There is a visual effect of a slight *stop* as viewed in profile.

The **muzzle** and **skull** are equal in length. The *muzzle* is well filled under the eyes with no visible cheek muscles. The underjaw is full and well defined and the **nose** is black.

Tight black *lips* lie close to the jaw. The jaws should be full and powerful with full and proper **dentition**. The teeth are white and strongly developed with a true scissors bite. Level bite is acceptable.

The Manchester Terrier's front legs are straight, always of proportionate length, and placed well under the brisket.

Neck, Topline, Body—The slightly arched **neck** should be slim and graceful, and of moderate length. It gradually becomes larger as it approaches, and blends smoothly with the sloping shoulders. Throatiness is undesirable.

The **topline** shows a slight arch over the robust loins falling slightly to the tail set. A flat back or roached back is to be severely penalized.

The *chest* is narrow between the legs and deep in the brisket. The forechest is moderately defined.

The *ribs* are well-sprung, but flattened in the lower end to permit clearance of the forelegs.

The *abdomen* should be tucked up extending in an arched line form the deep brisket.

The taper style **tail** is moderately short reaching no further then the hock joint. It is set on at the end of the croup. Being thicker where it joins the body, the tail tapers to a point. The tail is carried in a slight upward curve, but never over the back.

Forequarters—The *shoulder blades* and the *upper arm* should be relatively the same length. The distance from the elbow to the withers should be approximately the same as the distance from the elbow to the

The Manchester has a pleasing expression—keen, intelligent, and alert.

ground. The *elbows* should lie close to the brisket. The *shoulders* are well laid back. The *forelegs* are straight, of proportionate length, and placed well under the brisket. The pasterns should be almost perpendicular.

The **front feet** are compact and well arched. The two middle toes should be slightly longer than the others. The pads should be thick and the toenails should be jet black.

Hindquarters—The *thigh* should be muscular with the length of the upper and lower thighs being approximately equal. The stifle is well turned.

The well let down hocks should not turn in nor out as viewed from the rear. The hind legs are carried well back.

The **hind feet** are shaped like those of a cat with thick pads and jet black nails.

Coat—The coat should be smooth, short, dense, tight, and glossy; not soft.

Color—The coat color should be jet black and rich mahogany tan, which should not run or blend into each other, but abruptly form clear, well defined lines of color. There shall be a very small tan spot on each cheek. On the head, the muzzle is tanned to the nose.

The jet black and rich mahogany tan coat of the Manchester Terrier should be smooth, short, dense, and tight.

The nose and nasal bone are jet black. The tan extends under the throat, ending in the shape of the letter V. The inside of the ears are partly tan. There shall be tan spots, called "rosettes," on each side of the chest above the front legs. These are more pronounced in puppies than in adults. There should be a distinct black "pencil mark" line running lengthwise on the top of each toe on all four feet. Tan on the hind leg should continue from the penciling on the toes up the inside of the legs to a little below the stifle joint. The outside of the hind legs should be black. There should be tan under the tail, and on the vent, but only of such size as to be covered by the tail.

White on any part of the coat is a serious fault, and shall disqualify whenever the white shall form a patch of stripe measuring as much as one half inch at its longest dimension.

Any color other than black and tan shall be disqualified.

Color and/or markings should never take precedence over soundness and type.

The head of the Manchester is long, narrow, and almost flat.

Ch. Rosewood Aim For The Stars demonstrates what it takes to make a champion.

Gait—The gait should be free and effortless with good reach of the forequarters, showing no indication of hackney gait. Rear quarters should have strong, driving power to match the front reach. Hocks should fully extend. Each rear leg should move in line with the foreleg of the same side, neither thrown in nor out. When moving at a trot, the legs tend to converge towards the center of gravity line beneath the dog.

Temperament—The Manchester Terrier is neither aggressive nor shy. He is keenly observant, devoted, but discerning. Not being a sparring breed, the Manchester is generally very friendly with other dogs. Excessive shyness or aggressiveness should be considered a serious fault.

DISQUALIFICATIONS

Standard variety—Weight over 22 pounds.

Top variety—Cropped or cut ears.

Both varieties—White on any part of the coat whenever the white shall form a patch or stripe measuring as much as one half inch at its longest dimension.

Any color other than black and tan.

Approved June 10, 1991

Effective July 31, 1991

BREED REQUIREMENTS

ENVIRONMENT

The Manchester Terrier seems happy and well adjusted in just about any type of home. If you dwell in suburbia, your Manchester will be content to spend his days outdoors, basking in the sun, accompanying his family in work or play, or perhaps going about his own business of inspecting everything that grabs his attention. In the evenings, he will be content to spend his time in your presence while you quietly watch television or read the evening paper.

These two Manchester friends know that as long as they have each other, they can be comfortable anywhere!

BREED REQUIREMENTS

If your living conditions do not permit for outside time or you are a city dweller, have no fear. The Manchester Terrier will just as easily adjust to this lifestyle as any other. A small fenced-in yard is adequate, but not necessary. The Manchester will be just as content to take a long leisurely walk with you on his leash.

With this breed, however it is essential to provide a place that he can call his very own, a personal territory. This place, preferably a roomy crate, becomes a sanctuary where your Manchester Terrier can retreat from the world around him. Depending upon your dog, he may even choose to eat inside his crate. The crate should not be used as punishment or as a place to hide from the world. It will also serve as a means of security for your Manchester in situations where large groups of people are present, and if your dog becomes agitated, placing a light sheet over the crate will help him to settle down.

The Manchester Terrier is active and energetic and will benefit greatly from plenty of time outdoors to explore and play.

Remember that no matter your surroundings, the most important thing to your Manchester is you, his owner. The bond between you and your dog is far more important than any deluxe model crate or big new house. With your loving companionship, your Manchester Terrier will be able to adapt to almost any situation you have to offer.

EXERCISE

The Manchester Terrier came to prominence as a gentleman's dog. He was not one of the toy breeds bred to look pretty on the laps of the ladies of the day. This is an energetic little dog that needs activity. Therefore, it is imperative that you, his owner, provide it for him.

A fenced-in yard is not necessary for the breed's well-being because Manchester Terriers love to go for walks. Daily exercise is an important part of any dog's health. A long leisurely walk, at least once a day in the good weather, will help to keep your Manchester fit. Keep in mind that this fiercely intelligent individual needs new situations and surroundings to stimulate his thinking and keep him interested in life.

Manchester puppies are no strangers to mischief—always carefully supervise your little fellows when outdoors.

BREED REQUIREMENTS

As with any other breed, it is imperative that on your walks together your Manchester wears a collar and lead when outside. Manchester Terriers can be disturbingly impulsive at times. A loud noise or the sight of another animal can be all they need to go dashing wildly off in the other direction. Inevitably, this dangerous situation leads to heartache. A leash will allow you to retain control at all times. In the event that a mishap does occur and your Manchester gets loose, a collar with an identification tag will allow others to contact you if your dog is found.

If you do have access to a fenced-in yard, take advantage of it. Although the Manchester Terrier should in no way be considered an outside dog, he does need plenty of activity and fresh air. A game of chase or a full-out run in the yard will be a welcome addition to any Manchester's routine. You will surely be delighted watching your Manchester exercise, as the speed and elegance with which he moves are truly marvelous.

Manchester Terriers are very social creatures and need the company of others—this little fellow enjoys an outing with his family.

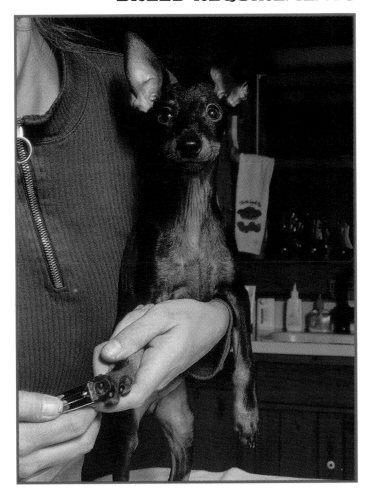

You must never ignore your Manchester's feet during grooming. Check for cracked footpads and keep his nails trimmed short to prevent injury.

HANDLING

All puppies are adorable and no one can resist the urge to pick them up and cuddle them. Manchester Terrier puppies are no different, and in the case of the Toy Manchester, they never grow out of it. It is important to remember that you must take care when lifting your dog. Never lift your dog by his front legs. Instead, support his whole body weight with both your hands. This will avoid stretching the Manchester Terrier's front leg muscles outward, which could easily result in a bow-legged dog.

GROOMING

The Manchester Terrier is a relatively maintenance free dog. He is fastidiously clean and does much of the work required for his upkeep, much like a cat. For your contribution, all you will need is the most basic of grooming accessories. A brush, a pair of electric clippers, scissors, nail clippers, and a toothbrush will be all you ever need to keep your Manchester Terrier looking spiffy at home or in the ring.

Grooming a Manchester requires nothing more than a brief daily inspection. Because brushing isn't necessary, simply wipe your dog down with a damp cloth. During this time, you should also examine your dog for any parasites or signs of illness. You may need to occasionally trim the hair around his footpads. His teeth should be brushed once a week and kept free of plaque build-up. It is a good idea to accustom your Manchester Terrier to nail clipping early on in life. Be careful not to cut the "quick" of the nail (the vein visible in each nail) when trimming or you will cause your dog pain and blood loss. Be sure to have some clotting preparation on hand, such as a styptic pencil, during the procedure in case of a mishap.

Because they are generally very clean animals, there is no need to bathe Manchester Terriers regularly. However, when the need does arise, it is important to keep in mind that they are sometimes prone to skin irritation. Be sure to use a shampoo specially formulated for a dog's sensitive skin, as well as a gentle conditioner to keep the coat shiny and soft.

If you accustom your Manchester Terrier to grooming procedures at an early age, he will come to think of it as a pleasant experience.

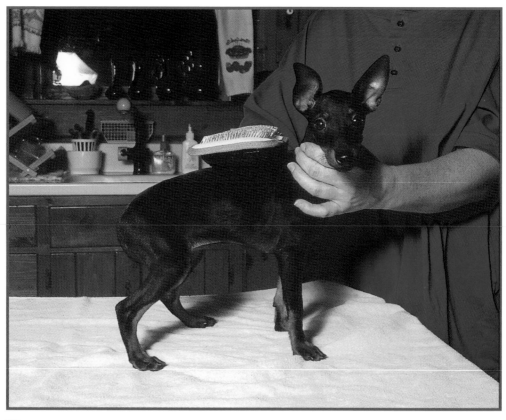

Your Manchester Terrier's relationship with other dogs is an essential one. This group of friends enjoys some outdoor playtime.

It is important to note that I have found that some dogs will suffer bad skin irritations if their bedding is washed in harsh detergent. I recommend using a gentle hand-washing soap to ensure that no such problems occur.

SOCIALIZATION

Dogs are pack animals. In the wild, they live in a strictly defined social system comprised of the pack leader and the surrounding hierarchy. Socialization is basically the process by which a puppy learns how to live harmoniously with other canine and human family members. This process is begun by the puppy's mother only days after birth. She diligently corrects any overly unruly behavior. By four weeks of age, your Manchester must be introduced to human contact and socialization begins. By about the fifth week of life, the puppy has developed to the point where more human socialization becomes increasingly important. Now and for the following few weeks, your Manchester Terrier will learn two different social codes: one for the human world and one for the canine world. It is

A young puppy will not know the difference between good and bad behavior. It is up to the leader of the pack to teach him—once he arrives home that will be your job.

extremely necessary that both of these occur, otherwise behavioral problems can result later in the dog's life.

Proper socialization provides the backbone for the human-dog relationship started by the breeder but truly determined by you. It is of the utmost importance that you keep this in mind, for all of your Manchester Terrier's future interactions will be affected by the groundwork you lay in his first few weeks in your home. Introduce your puppy to as many different people and situations as possible—the more people he meets, the better socialized he will become. The

Bonding is by far one of the most important building blocks of socialization. This little Manchester revels in the love and attention he gets from his owner.

Consult your breeder or veterinarian about the appropriate diet for your Manchester Terrier.

housebreaking and basic training methods you use help establish the lifelong relationship for you and your Manchester Terrier. Socialization techniques must always take into account the individual dog as well as his breed type. Certain breeds of dog will respond to certain methods better than others. This is best determined by your breeder who should be able to offer invaluable advice. As for your individual animal, all Manchester Terriers have personalities of their own. You will quickly realize there are certain ways to interact with your dog that will be unique unto the two of you.

FEEDING

You may want to feed your Manchester Terrier freshly prepared food if you have the time and inclination to do so. I have found that they do not digest beef well. Chicken and rice mixed with a quality   dry food is excellent. Dry food is also important to teething puppies. Oftentimes, they will chew dry food to alleviate the pain of teething. It is also important during teething that you observe your Manchester Terrier puppy's diet. A mixture of rice cereal, chicken baby food, and water or goat's milk will be easily swallowed without a lot of chewing and provide the nutrition necessary for your puppy's proper growth.

Also, remember to make water available to your Manchester Terrier at all times. Because they are small dogs, they can become dehydrated very easily. Dehydration can be an extremely dangerous condition that is often accompanied by fever and, in extreme cases, can lead to death.

HOUSEBREAKING

Aside from the conventional methods of housebreaking, I have had excellent results, especially with Toy Manchester Terriers, using the following method. Obtain a flat metal or sturdy plastic pan, similar to a large baking pan or litter box. Fill the

It is important to have cool, clean water available to your Manchester at all times.

During housetraining, allow your puppy plenty of time outdoors to attend to his needs.

bottom half with kitty litter and the top half with pine wood shavings or shredded paper (which they adore). The pan should be at least three inches high and two and one-half feet wide, possibly a little larger. Each time your puppy begins to circle and sniff the ground, pick him up and place him in the pan. Soon, he will learn to use the pan for his needs without prompting from you. Once he has accomplished this, move the pan steadily toward the door, a little more each day. Finally, you will be able to move the pan outside. Your puppy has now learned that you prefer him to relieve himself outdoors. After several days, remove the pan. He will continue to go outdoors to look for it. When he cannot locate the pan, he will choose his own spot in which to take care of his needs, probably not far from where the pan used to reside—keep this in mind when placing it outdoors. Using this method, you will have a well-housetrained Manchester Terrier puppy in no time!

YOUR PUPPY'S NEW HOME

Before actually collecting your puppy, it is better that you purchase the basic items you will need in advance of the pup's arrival date. This allows you more opportunity to shop around and ensure you have exactly what you want rather than having to buy lesser quality in a hurry.

It is always better to collect the puppy as early in the day as possible. In most instances this will mean that the puppy has a few hours with your family before it is time to retire for his first night's sleep away from his former home.

Be sure to do your homework and learn all you can about the breed before making the decision to bring a Manchester into your home.

If the breeder is local, then you may not need any form of box to place the puppy in when you bring him home. A member of the family can hold the pup in his lap—duly protected by some towels just in case the puppy becomes car sick! Be sure to advise the breeder at what time you hope to arrive for the puppy, as this will obviously influence the feeding of the pup that morning or afternoon. If you arrive early in the day, then they will likely only give the pup a light breakfast so as to reduce the risk of travel sickness.

If the trip will be of a few hours duration, you should take a travel crate with you. The crate will provide your pup with a safe place to lie down and rest during the trip. During the trip, the puppy will no doubt wish to relieve his bowels, so you will have to make a few

If you are traveling a long distance to bring your puppy home, allow for frequent stops during the trip so he can exercise and relieve himself.

stops. On a long journey you may need a rest yourself, and can take the opportunity to let the puppy get some fresh air. However, do not let the puppy walk where there may have been a lot of other dogs because he might pick up an infection. Also, if he relieves his bowels at such a time, do not just leave the feces where they were dropped. This is the height of irresponsibility. It has resulted in many public parks and other places actually banning dogs. You can purchase poop-scoops from your pet shop and should have them with you whenever you are taking the dog out where he might foul a public place.

Your journey home should be made as quickly as possible. If it is a hot day, be sure the car interior is amply supplied with fresh air. It should never be too hot or too cold for the puppy. The pup must never be placed where he might be subject to a draft. If the journey requires an overnight stop at a motel, be aware that other guests will not appreciate a puppy crying half the night. You must regard the puppy as a baby and comfort him so he does not cry for long periods. The worst thing you can do is to shout at or smack him. This will mean your relationship is off to a really bad start. You wouldn't smack a baby, and your puppy is still very much just this.

ON ARRIVING HOME

By the time you arrive home the puppy may be very tired, in which case he should be taken to his sleeping area and allowed to rest. Children should not be allowed to interfere with the pup when he is sleeping. If the pup is not tired, he can be allowed to investigate his new home—but always under your close supervision. After a short look around, the puppy will no doubt appreciate a light meal and a drink of water. Do not overfeed him at his first meal because he will be in an excited state and more likely to be sick.

Although it is an obvious temptation, you should not invite friends and neighbors around to see the new arrival until he has had at least 48 hours in which to settle down. Indeed, if you can delay this longer then do so, especially if the puppy is not fully

The Manchester Terrier puppy you choose should be bright-eyed, healthy, and interested in the world around him.

Your Manchester Terrier will look to you, his owner, to provide for all his needs. It is important that he has regular veterinary check-ups and inoculations.

vaccinated. At the very least, the visitors might introduce some local bacteria on their clothing that the puppy is not immune to. This aspect is always a risk when a pup has been moved some distance, so the fewer people the pup meets in the first week or so the better.

DANGERS IN THE HOME

Your home holds many potential dangers for a little mischievous puppy, so you must think about these in advance and be sure he is protected from them. The more obvious are as follows:

Open Fires. All open fires should be protected by a mesh screen guard so there is no danger of the pup being burned by spitting pieces of coal or wood.

Electrical Wires. Puppies just love chewing on things, so be sure that all electrical appliances are neatly hidden from view and are not left plugged in when not in use. It is not sufficient simply to turn the plug switch to the off position—pull the plug from the socket.

Open Doors. A door would seem a pretty innocuous object, yet with a strong draft it could kill or injure a puppy easily if it is slammed shut. Always ensure there is no risk of this happening. It is most likely during warm weather when you have windows or outside doors open and a sudden gust of wind blows through.

Balconies. If you live in a high-rise building, obviously the pup must be protected from falling. Be sure he cannot get through any railings on your patio, balcony, or deck.

Ponds and Pools. A garden pond or a swimming pool is a very dangerous place for a little puppy to be near. Be sure it is well screened so there is no risk of the pup falling in. It takes barely a minute for a pup— or a child—to drown.

The Kitchen. While many puppies will be kept in the kitchen, at least while they are toddlers and not able to control their bowel movements, this is a room full of danger—especially while you are cooking. When cooking, keep the puppy in a play pen or in another room where he is safely out of harm's way. Alternatively, if you have a carry box or crate, put him in this so he can still see you but is well protected.

Be aware, when using washing machines, that more than one puppy has clambered in and decided

Puppies love to chew on things, so make sure that all electrical appliances are neatly hidden from view and unplugged when not in use.

to have a nap and received a wash instead! If you leave the washing machine door open and leave the room for any reason, then be sure to check inside the machine before you close the door and switch on.

Small Children. Toddlers and small children should never be left unsupervised with puppies. In spite of such advice it is amazing just how many people not only do this but also allow children to pull and maul pups. They should be taught from the outset that a puppy is not a plaything to be dragged about the home—and they should be promptly scolded if they disobey.

Children must be shown how to lift a puppy so it is safe. Failure by you to correctly educate your children about dogs could one day result in their getting a very nasty bite or scratch. When a puppy is lifted, his weight must always be supported. To lift the pup, first place your right hand under his chest. Next, secure the pup by using your left hand to hold his neck. Now you can lift him and bring him close to your chest. Never lift a pup by his ears and, while he can be lifted by the scruff of his neck where the fur is loose, there is no reason ever to do this, so don't.

Manchester Terriers love snacks, but they must learn never to help themselves.

When picking up your puppy, be careful to support his body weight evenly in order to prevent injury.

Beyond the dangers already cited you may be able to think of other ones that are specific to your home—steep basement steps or the like. Go around your home and check out all potential problems—you'll be glad you did.

THE FIRST NIGHT

The first few nights a puppy spends away from his mother and littermates are quite traumatic for him. He will feel very lonely, maybe cold, and will certainly miss the heartbeat of his siblings when sleeping. To help overcome his loneliness it may help to place a clock next to his bed—one with a loud tick. This will in some way soothe him, as the clock ticks to a rhythm not dissimilar from a heart beat. A cuddly toy or a radio playing soft music may also help in the first few weeks. A dim nightlight may provide some comfort to the puppy, because his eyes will not yet be fully able to see in the dark. The puppy may want to leave his bed for a drink or to relieve himself.

If the pup does whimper in the night, there are two things you should not do. One is to get up and chastise him, because he will not understand why you are shouting at him; and the other is to rush to comfort him every time he cries because he will quickly realize that

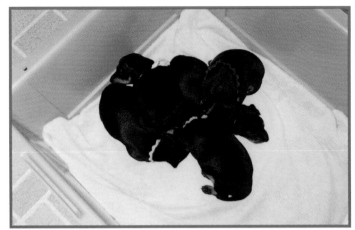

In your puppy's early life he probably slept with his littermates. On his first few nights in your home he'll need plenty of love and attention to keep from feeling lonely.

if he wants you to come running all he needs to do is to holler loud enough!

By all means give your puppy some extra attention on his first night, but after this quickly refrain from so doing. The pup will cry for a while but then settle down and go to sleep. Some pups are, of course, worse than others in this respect, so you must use balanced judgment in the matter. Many owners take their pups to bed with them, and there is certainly nothing wrong with this.

The pup will be no trouble in such cases. However, you should only do this if you intend to let this be a permanent arrangement, otherwise it is hardly fair to the puppy. If you have decided to have two puppies, then they will keep each other company and you will have few problems.

OTHER PETS

If you have other pets in the home then the puppy must be introduced to them under careful supervision. Puppies will get on just fine with any other pets—but you must make due allowance for the respective sizes of the pets concerned, and appreciate that your puppy has a rather playful nature. It would be very foolish to leave him with a young rabbit. The pup will want to play and might bite the bunny and get altogether too rough with it. Kittens are more able to defend themselves from overly cheeky pups, who will get a quick scratch if they overstep the mark. The adult cat could obviously give the pup a very bad scratch, though generally cats will jump clear of pups and watch them from a suitable vantage point. Eventually they will meet at ground level where the cat will quickly hiss and box a puppy's ears. The pup will soon learn to respect an adult cat; thereafter they will probably develop into great friends as the pup matures into an adult dog.

HOUSETRAINING

Undoubtedly, the first form of training your puppy will undergo is in respect to his toilet habits. To achieve this you can use either newspaper, or a large litter tray filled with soil or lined with newspaper. A puppy cannot control his bowels until he is a few months old, and not fully until he is an adult. Therefore you must anticipate his needs and be prepared for a few accidents. The prime times a pup will urinate and defecate are shortly after he wakes up from a sleep, shortly after he has eaten, and after he has been playing awhile. He will usually whimper and start searching the room for a suitable place. You must quickly pick him up and place him on the newspaper or in the litter tray. Hold him in position gently but firmly. He might jump out of the box without doing anything on the first one or two occasions, but if you simply repeat the procedure every time you think he wants to relieve himself then eventually he will get the message.

When he does defecate as required, give him plenty of praise, telling him what a good puppy he is. The litter tray or newspaper must, of course, be cleaned or replaced after each use—puppies do not like using a dirty toilet any more than you do. The pup's toilet can be placed near the kitchen door and as he gets older the

Housebreaking your puppy successfully relies on your patience and consistent reinforcement.

Your Manchester Terrier is happiest when being loved and enjoyed. With patience, persistence, and praise, he will become a well-trained and obedient companion for life.

tray can be placed outside while the door is open. The pup will then start to use it while he is outside. From that time on, it is easy to get the pup to use a given area of the yard.

Many breeders recommend the popular alternative of crate training. Upon bringing the pup home, introduce him to his crate. The crate is the best choice, placed in a restricted, draft-free area of the home. Put the pup's Nylabone® and other favorite toys in the crate along with a wool blanket or other suitable bedding. The puppy's natural cleanliness instincts prohibit him from soiling in the place where he sleeps, his crate. The puppy should be allowed to go in and out of the open crate during the day, but he should sleep in the crate at the night and at other intervals during the day. Whenever the pup is taken out of his crate, he should be brought outside (or to his newspapers) to do his business. Never use the crate as a place of punishment. You will see how quickly your pup takes to his crate, considering it as his own safe haven from the big world around him.

THE EARLY DAYS

You will no doubt be given much advice on how to bring up your puppy. This will come from dog-owning friends, neighbors, and through articles and books you may read on the subject. Some of the advice will be sound, some will be nothing short of rubbish. What you should do above all else is to keep an open mind and let common sense prevail over prejudice and worn-out ideas that have been handed down over the centuries. There is no one way that is superior to all others, no more than there is no one dog that is exactly a replica of another. Each is an individual and must always be regarded as such.

A dog never becomes disobedient, unruly, or a menace to society without the full consent of his owner. Your puppy may have many limitations, but the singular biggest limitation he is confronted with in so many instances is his owner's inability to understand his needs and how to cope with them.

IDENTIFICATION

It is a sad reflection on our society that the number of dogs and cats stolen every year runs into many thousands. To these can be added the number that get lost. If you do not want your cherished pet to be lost or stolen, then you should see that he is carrying a permanent identification number, as well as a temporary tag on his collar.

Permanent markings come in the form of tattoos placed either inside the pup's ear flap, or on the inner side of a pup's upper rear leg. The number given is then recorded with one of the national registration compa-

Make sure your Manchester Terrier wears a collar with tags when outside. This will increase your chances of being reunited should you become separated.

The newest method of identification is the microchip, a computer chip that is no bigger than a grain of rice, which is injected into the dog's skin.

nies. Research laboratories will not purchase dogs carrying numbers as they realize these are clearly someone's pet, and not abandoned animals. As a result, thieves will normally abandon dogs so marked and this at least gives the dog a chance to be taken to the police or the dog pound, when the number can be traced and the dog reunited with its family. The only problem with this method at this time is that there are a number of registration bodies, so it is not always apparent which one the dog is registered with (as you provide the actual number). However, each registration body is aware of his competitors and will normally be happy to supply their addresses. Those holding the dog can check out which one you are with. It is not a perfect system, but until such is developed it's the best available.

Another permanent form of identification is the microchip, a computer chip that is no bigger than a grain of rice that is injected between the dog's shoulder blades. The dog feels no discomfort. The dog also receives a tag that says he is microchipped. If the dog is lost and picked up by the humane society, they can trace the owner by scanning the microchip. It is the safest form of identification.

A temporary tag takes the form of a metal or plastic disk large enough for you to place the dog's name and your phone number on it—maybe even your address as well. In virtually all places you will be required to obtain a license for your puppy. This may not become applicable until the pup is six months old, but it might apply regardless of his age. Much depends upon the state within a country, or the country itself, so check with your veterinarian if the breeder has not already advised you on this.

FEEDING YOUR MANCHESTER TERRIER

Dog owners today are fortunate in that they live in an age when considerable cash has been invested in the study of canine nutritional requirements. This means dog food manufacturers are very concerned about ensuring that their foods are of the best quality. The result of all of their studies, apart from the food itself, is that dog owners are bombarded with advertisements telling them why they must purchase a given brand. The number of products avail-

Puppies grow very quickly and require especially nutritious meals to grow into healthy adults.

able to you is unlimited, so it is hardly surprising to find that dogs in general suffer from obesity and an excess of vitamins, rather than the reverse. Be sure to feed age-appropriate food—puppy food up to one year of age, adult food thereafter. Generally breeders recommend dry food supplemented by canned, if needed.

FACTORS AFFECTING NUTRITIONAL NEEDS

Activity Level. A dog that lives in a country environment and is able to exercise for long periods of the day will need more food than the same breed of dog living in an apartment and given little exercise.

Quality of the Food. Obviously the quality of food will affect the quantity required by a puppy. If the nutritional content of a food is low then the puppy will need more of it than if a better quality food was fed.

Balance of Nutrients and Vitamins. Feeding a puppy the correct balance of nutrients is not easy because the average person is not able to measure out ratios of one to another, so it is a case of trying to see that nothing is in excess. However, only tests, or your veterinarian, can be the source of reliable advice.

Genetic and Biological Variation. Apart from all of the other considerations, it should be remem-

It is important to feed your Manchester Terrier a well-balanced diet in order to keep him healthy and happy.

bered that each puppy is an individual. His genetic make-up will influence not only his physical characteristics but also his metabolic efficiency. This being so, two pups from the same litter can vary quite a bit in the amount of food they need to perform the same function under the same conditions. If you consider the potential combinations of all of these factors then you will see that pups of a given breed could vary quite a bit in the amount of food they will need. Before discussing feeding quantities it is valuable to know at least a little about the composition of food and its role in the body.

COMPOSITION AND ROLE OF FOOD

The main ingredients of food are protein, fats, and carbohydrates, each of which is needed in relatively large quantities when compared to the other needs of vitamins and minerals. The other vital ingredient of food is, of course, water. Although all foods obviously contain some of the basic ingredients needed for an animal to survive, they do not all contain the ingredients in the needed ratios or type. For example, there are many forms of protein, just as there are many types of carbohydrates. Both of these compounds are found in meat and in vegetable matter—but not all of those that are needed will be in one particular meat or vegetable. Plants, especially, do not contain certain amino acids that are required for the synthesis of certain proteins needed by dogs.

Likewise, vitamins are found in meats and vegetable matter, but vegetables are a richer source of most. Meat contains very little carbohydrates. Some vitamins can be synthesized by the dog, so do not need to be supplied via the food. Dogs are carnivores and this means their digestive tract has evolved to need a high quantity of meat as compared to humans. The digestive system of carnivores is unable to break down the tough cellulose walls of plant matter, but it is easily able to assimilate proteins from meat.

In order to gain its needed vegetable matter in a form that it can cope with, the carnivore eats all of its prey. This includes the partly digested food within the stomach. In commercially prepared foods, the cellulose is broken down by cooking. During this process the vitamin content is either greatly reduced or lost altogether. The manufacturer therefore adds vitamins once the heat process has been

There are a number of quality dog foods and treats available that will offer special nutritional value to your Manchester Terrier.

completed. This is why commercial foods are so useful as part of a feeding regimen, providing they are of good quality and from a company that has prepared the foods very carefully.

Proteins

These are made from amino acids, of which at least ten are essential if a puppy is to maintain healthy growth. Proteins provide the building blocks for the puppy's body. The richest sources are meat, fish and poultry, together with their by-products. The latter will include milk, cheese, yogurt, fishmeal, and eggs. Vegetable matter that has a high protein content includes soy beans, together with numerous corn and other plant extracts that have been dehydrated. The actual protein content needed in the diet will be determined both by the activity level of the dog and his age. The total protein need will also be influenced by the digestibility factor of the food given.

Fats

These serve numerous roles in the puppy's body. They provide insulation against the cold, and help buffer the organs from knocks and general activity shocks. They provide the richest source of energy, and reserves of this, and they are vital in the transport of vitamins and other nutrients, via the blood, to all other organs. Finally, it is the fat content within a diet that gives it palatability. It is important that the fat content of a diet should not be excessive. This is because the high energy content of fats (more than twice that of protein or carbohydrate) will increase the overall energy content of the diet. The puppy will adjust its food intake to that of its energy needs, which are obviously more easily met in a high-energy diet. This will mean that while the fats are providing the energy needs of the puppy, the overall diet may not be providing its protein, vitamin, and mineral needs, so signs of protein deficiency will become apparent. Rich sources of fats are meat, their byproducts (butter, milk), and vegetable oils, such as safflower, olive, corn or soy bean.

Carbohydrates

These are the principal energy compounds given to puppies and adult dogs. Their inclusion within most commercial brand dog foods is for cost, rather than dietary needs. These compounds are more commonly known as sugars, and they are seen in simple or complex compounds of carbon, hydrogen, and oxygen. One of the simple sugars is called glucose, and it is vital to many metabolic processes. When large chains of glucose are created, they form compound sugars. One of these is called glycogen, and it is found in the cells of animals. Another, called starch, is the material that is found in the cells of plants.

Vitamins

These are not foods as such but chemical compounds that assist in all aspects of an animal's life. They help in so many ways that to attempt to describe these effectively would require a chapter in itself. Fruits are a rich source of vitamins, as is the liver of most animals. Many vitamins are unstable and easily destroyed by light, heat, moisture, or rancidity. An excess of vitamins, especially A and D, has been proven to be very harmful. Provided a puppy is receiving a balanced diet, it is most unlikely there will be a deficiency, whereas hypervitaminosis (an excess of vitamins) has become quite common due to owners and breeders feeding unneeded supplements. The only time you should feed extra vitamins to your puppy is if your veterinarian advises you to.

Minerals

These provide strength to bone and cell tissue, as well as assist in many metabolic processes. Examples are calcium, phosphorous, copper, iron, magnesium, selenium, potassium, zinc, and sodium. The recommended amounts of all minerals in the diet has not been fully established. Calcium and phosphorous are known to be important, especially to puppies. They help in forming strong bone. As with vitamins, a mineral deficiency is most unlikely in pups given a good and varied diet. Again, an excess can create problems—this applying equally to calcium.

Water

This is the most important of all nutrients, as is easily shown by the fact that the adult dog is made up of about 60 percent water, the puppy containing an even higher percentage. Dogs must retain a water balance, which means that the total intake should be balanced by the total output. The intake comes either by direct input (the tap or its equivalent), plus water released when food is oxidized, known as metabolic water (remember that all foods

Clean water is essential to your dog's good health— this little guy reaches in and gives himself a hand.

contain the elements hydrogen and oxygen that recombine in the body to create water). A dog without adequate water will lose condition more rapidly than one depleted of food, a fact common to most animal species.

AMOUNT TO FEED

The best way to determine dietary requirements is by observing the puppy's general health and physical appearance. If he is well covered with flesh, shows good bone development and muscle, and is an active alert puppy, then his diet is fine. A puppy will consume about twice as much as an adult (of the same breed). You should ask the breeder of your puppy to show you the amounts fed to their pups and this will be a good starting point.

The puppy should eat his meal in about five to seven minutes. Any leftover food can be discarded or placed into the refrigerator until the next meal (but be sure it is thawed fully if your fridge is very cold).

If the puppy quickly devours its meal and is clearly still hungry, then you are not giving him enough food. If he eats readily but then begins to pick at it, or walks away leaving a quantity, then you are probably giving him too much food. Adjust this at the next meal and you will quickly begin to appreciate what the correct amount is. If, over a number of weeks, the pup starts to look fat, then he is obviously overeating; the reverse is true if he starts to look thin compared with others of the same breed.

WHEN TO FEED

It really does not matter what times of the day the puppy is fed, as long as he receives the needed quantity of food. Puppies from 8 weeks to 12 or 16 weeks need 3 or 4 meals a day. Older puppies and adult dogs should be fed twice a day. What is most important is that the feeding times are reasonably regular. They can be tailored to fit in with your own timetable—for example, 7 a.m. and 6 p.m. The dog will then expect his meals at these times each day. Keeping regular feeding times and feeding set amounts will help you monitor your puppy's or dog's health. If a dog that's normally enthusiastic about mealtimes and eats readily suddenly shows a lack of interest in food, you'll know something's not right.

TRAINING YOUR MANCHESTER TERRIER

Successful showing requires dedication and preparation, but most of all, it should be an enjoyable experience for handlers and dogs alike. Ch. Rosewood Pride shows us how it's done.

Once your puppy has settled into your home and responds to his name, then you can begin his basic training. Before giving advice on how you should go about doing this, two important points should be made. You should train the puppy in isolation of any potential distractions, and you should keep all lessons very short. It is essential that you have the full

attention of your puppy. This is not possible if there are other people about, or televisions and radios on, or other pets in the vicinity. Even when the pup has become a young adult, the maximum time you should allocate to a lesson is about 20 minutes. However, you can give the puppy more than one lesson a day, three being as many as are recommended, each well spaced apart.

Before beginning a lesson, always play a little game with the puppy so he is in an active state of mind and thus more receptive to the matter at hand. Likewise, always end a lesson with fun-time for the pup, and always—this is most important—end on a high note, praising the puppy and giving a treat. Let the lesson end when the pup has done as you require so he receives lots of fuss. This will really build his confidence.

COLLAR AND LEASH TRAINING

Training a puppy to his collar and leash is very easy. Place a collar on the puppy and, although he will initially try to bite at it, he will soon forget it, the more so if you play with him. You can leave the collar on for a few hours. Some people leave their dogs' collars on all of the time, others only when they are taking the dog out. If it is to be left on, purchase a narrow or round one so it does not mark the fur.

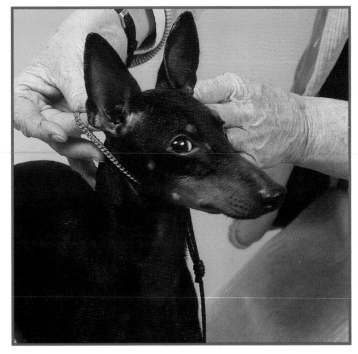

The first step toward a well-trained dog is familiarizing him with his collar and lead.

This alert Manchester Terrier eagerly awaits his owner's next command.

Once the puppy ignores his collar, then you can attach the leash to it and let the puppy pull this along behind it for a few minutes. However, if the pup starts to chew at the leash, simply hold the leash but keep it slack and let the pup go where he wants. The idea is to let him get the feel of the leash, but not get in the habit of chewing it. Repeat this a couple of times a day for two days and the pup will get used to the leash without thinking that it will restrain him—which you will not have attempted to do yet.

Next, you can let the pup understand that the leash will restrict his movements. The first time he realizes this, he will pull and buck or just sit down. Immediately call the pup to you and give him lots of fuss. Never tug on the leash so the puppy is dragged along the floor, as this simply implants a negative thought in his mind.

THE COME COMMAND

Come is the most vital of all commands and especially so for the independently minded dog. To teach the puppy to come, let him reach the end of a long lead, then give the command and his name, gently pulling him toward you at the same time. As soon as he associates the word come with the action of moving toward you, pull only when he does not respond immediately. As he starts to come, move back to make him learn that he must come from a distance as well as when he is close to you. Soon you may be able to practice without a leash, but if he is slow to come or notably disobedient, go to him and pull him toward you, repeating the command. Never scold a dog during this exercise—or any other exercise. Remember the trick is that the puppy must want to come to you. For the very independent dog, hand signals may work better than verbal commands.

THE SIT COMMAND

As with most basic commands, your puppy will learn this one in just a few lessons. You can give the puppy two lessons a day on the sit command but he will make just as much progress with one 15-minute lesson each day. Some trainers will advise you that you should not proceed to other commands until the previous one has been learned really well. However, a bright young pup is quite capable of handling more

The time you invest in training your Manchester will benefit the both of you for a lifetime.

With the aid of your Manchester's favorite treat, he'll be obeying commands in no time.

than one command per lesson, and certainly per day. Indeed, as time progresses, you will be going through each command as a matter of routine before a new one is attempted. This is so the puppy always starts, as well as ends, a lesson on a high note, having successfully completed something.

Call the puppy to you and fuss over him. Place one hand on his hindquarters and the other under his upper chest. Say "Sit" in a pleasant (never harsh) voice. At the same time, push down his rear end and push up under his chest. Now lavish praise on the puppy. Repeat this a few times and your pet will get the idea. Once the puppy is in the sit position you will release your hands. At first he will tend to get up, so immediately repeat the exercise. The lesson will end when the pup is in the sit position. When the puppy understands the command, and does it right away, you can slowly move backwards so that you are a few feet away from him. If he attempts to come to you, simply place him back in the original position and start again. Do not attempt to keep the pup in the sit position for too long. At this age, even a few seconds is a long while and you do not want him to get bored with lessons before he has even begun them.

THE HEEL COMMAND

All dogs should be able to walk nicely on a leash without their owners being involved in a tug-of-war. The heel command will follow leash training. Heel training is best done where you have a wall to one side of you. This will restrict the puppy's lateral movements, so you only have to contend with forward and backward situations. A fence is an alternative, or you can do the lesson in the garage. Again, it is better to do the lesson in private, not on a public sidewalk where there will be many distractions.

With a puppy, there will be no need to use a choke collar as you can be just as effective with a regular one. The leash should be of good length, certainly not too short. You can adjust the space between you, the puppy, and the wall so your pet has only a small amount of room to move sideways. This being so, he will either hang back or pull ahead—the latter is the more desirable state as it indicates a bold pup who is not frightened of you.

Hold the leash in your right hand and pass it through your left. As the puppy moves ahead and strains on the leash, give the leash a quick jerk backwards with your left hand, at the same time saying "Heel." The position you want the pup to be in is such that his chest is level with, or just behind, an imaginary line from your knee. When the puppy is in this position, praise him and begin walking again, and the whole exercise will be repeated. Once the puppy begins to get the message, you can use your left hand to pat the side of your knee so the pup is encouraged to keep close to your side.

It is useful to suddenly do an about-turn when the pup understands the basics. The puppy will now be behind you, so you can pat your knee and say "Heel." As soon as the pup is in the correct position, give him lots of praise. The puppy will now be beginning to associate certain words with certain actions. Whenever he is not in the heel position he will experience displeasure as you jerk the leash, but when he comes alongside you he will receive praise. Given these two options, he will always prefer the latter—assuming he has no other reason to fear you, which would then create a dilemma in his mind.

Once the lesson has been well learned, then you can adjust your pace from a slow walk to a quick one and the puppy will come to adjust. The slow walk is always the more difficult for most puppies, as they are usually anxious to be on the move.

If you have no wall to walk against then things will be a little more difficult because the pup will tend to wander to his left. This means you need to give lateral jerks as well as bring the pup to your side. End the lesson when the pup is walking nicely beside you. Begin the lesson with a few sit commands (which he understands by now), so you're starting with success and praise. If your puppy is nervous on the leash, you should never drag him to your side as you may see so many other people do (who obviously didn't invest in a good book like you did!). If the pup sits down, call him to your side and give lots of praise. The pup must always come to you because he wants to. If he is dragged to your side he will see you doing the dragging—a big negative. When he races ahead he does not see you jerk the leash, so all he knows is that something restricted his movement and, once he was in a given position, you gave him lots of praise. This is using canine psychology to your advantage.

Always try to remember that if a dog must be disciplined, then try not to let him associate the discipline with you. This is not possible in all matters but, where it is, this is definitely to be preferred.

THE STAY COMMAND

This command follows from the sit. Face the puppy and say "Sit." Now step backwards, and as you do,

It is important to remember that your Manchester Terrier wants to please you and learn what you have to teach him. These three buddies practice the stay command.

say "Stay." Let the pup remain in the position for only a few seconds before calling him to you and giving lots of praise. Repeat this, but step further back. You do not need to shout at the puppy. Your pet is not deaf; in fact, his hearing is far better than yours. Speak just loudly enough for the pup to hear, yet use a firm voice. You can stretch the word to form a "sta-a-a-y." If the pup gets up and comes to you simply lift him up, place him back in the original position, and start again. As the pup comes to understand the command, you can move further and further back.

The next test is to walk away after placing the pup. This will mean your back is to him, which will tempt him to follow you. Keep an eye over your shoulder, and the minute the pup starts to move, spin around and, using a sterner voice, say either "Sit" or "Stay." If the pup has gotten quite close to you, then, again, return him to the original position.

As the weeks go by you can increase the length of time the pup is left in the stay position—but two to three minutes is quite long enough for a puppy. If your puppy drops into a lying position and is clearly more comfortable, there is nothing wrong with this. Likewise, your pup will want to face the direction in which you walked off. Some trainers will insist that the dog faces the direction he was placed in, regardless of whether you move off on his blind side. I have never believed in this sort of obedience because it has no practical benefit.

THE DOWN COMMAND

From the puppy's viewpoint, the down command can be one of the more difficult ones to accept. This is because the position is one taken up by a submissive dog in a wild pack situation. A timid dog will roll over— a natural gesture of submission. A bolder pup will want to get up, and might back off, not feeling he should have to submit to this command. He will feel that he is under attack from you and about to be punished—which is what would be the position in his natural environment. Once he comes to understand this is not the case, he will accept this unnatural position without any problem.

You may notice that some dogs will sit very quickly, but will respond to the down command more slowly—it is their way of saying that they will obey the command, but under protest!

There two ways to teach this command. One is, in my mind, more intimidating than the other, but it is up to you to decide which one works best for you. The first method is to stand in front of your puppy and bring him to the sit position, with his collar and leash on. Pass the leash under your left foot so that when you pull on it, the result is that the pup's neck is forced downwards. With your free left hand, push the pup's shoulders down while at the same time saying "Down." This is when a bold pup will instantly try to back off and wriggle in full protest. Hold the pup firmly by the shoulders so he stays in the position for a second or two, then tell him what a good dog he is and give him lots of praise. Repeat this only a few times in a lesson because otherwise the puppy will get bored and upset over this command. End with an easy command that brings back the pup's confidence.

The second method, and the one I prefer, is done as follows: Stand in front of the pup and then tell him to sit. Now kneel down, which is immediately far less intimidating to the puppy than to have you towering above him. Take each of his front legs and pull them

Dogs often jump up as a sign of affection. However, your Manchester Terrier must learn that not everyone will appreciate paw prints on their clothes!

forward, at the same time saying "Down." Release the legs and quickly apply light pressure on the shoulders with your left hand. Then, as quickly, say "Good boy" and give lots of fuss. Repeat two or three times only. The pup will learn over a few lessons. Remember, this is a very submissive act on the pup's behalf, so there is no need to rush matters.

RECALL TO HEEL COMMAND

When your puppy is coming to the heel position from an off-leash situation—such as if he has been running free—he should do this in the correct manner. He should pass behind you and take up his position and then sit. To teach this command, have the pup in front of you in the sit position with his collar and leash on. Hold the leash in your right hand. Give him the command to heel, and pat your left knee. As the pup starts to move forward, use your right hand to guide him behind you. If need be you can hold his collar and walk the dog around the back of you to the desired position. You will need to repeat this a few times until the dog understands what is wanted.

When he has done this a number of times, you can try it without the collar and leash. If the pup comes up toward your left side, then bring him to the sit position in front of you, hold his collar and walk him around the back of you. He will eventually understand and automatically pass around your back each time. If the dog is already behind you when you recall him, then he should automatically come to your left side, which you will be patting with your hand.

THE NO COMMAND

This is a command that must be obeyed every time without fail. There are no halfway stages, he must be 100-percent reliable. Most delinquent dogs have never been taught this command; included in these are the jumpers, the barkers, and the biters. Were your puppy to approach a poisonous snake or any other potential danger, the no command, coupled with the recall, could save his life. You do not need to give a specific lesson for this command because it will crop up time and again in day-to-day life.

If the puppy is chewing a slipper, you should approach the pup, take hold of the slipper, and say "No" in a stern voice. If he jumps onto the furniture, lift him off and say "No" and place him gently on the floor. You must be consistent in the use of the command and apply it every time he is doing something you do not want him to do.

HEALTH CONCERNS OF THE MANCHESTER TERRIER

THE MANCHESTER PUPPY'S BIRTH AND DEVELOPMENT

This tiny Manchester is only hours old. A healthy puppy is plump and content right from birth.

The newborn puppies of both the Standard Manchester Terrier and the Toy Manchester Terrier are extremely similar. At birth, they are the same size, five to six ounces, not even one-half pound. Generally, the dam does not need assistance during the birthing process, unless she is an exceptionally small Toy bitch, and then some difficulties may arise. It is important that the breeder remain close at hand, watchful yet unobtrusive.

As a responsible Manchester Terrier owner, you should have a basic understanding of the medical conditions that may effect the breed.

The whelping area that you provide should be kept quite warm, at around 80 degrees F, and slightly darkened quarters will help to ease the dam's excitability, especially with young mothers. After the birth of each puppy, the Manchester Terrier mother will vigorously clean her pup. Be sure that the placenta is passed for each puppy born. The mother may eat some or all of the placenta—this is not unusual and is said to offer special nutrients to the weakened dam.

The newborn Manchester Terrier will appear to be solid black, with few or no tan markings. The tan markings should develop in their proper areas over the first three to four weeks of life. Any mismarkings should be evident at birth or within a few days thereafter. Once your Manchester Terrier puppies are three to five days old, their dewclaws should be removed. The tails of both the Standard and Toy variety are left natural.

One of the greatest differences between the Standard and Toy Manchester Terrier concerns ear carriage. The ears of the Toy Manchester Terrier must not be surgically elevated or cropped. Your dog will raise his ears when he is ready, anywhere from three weeks to five to six months. If your puppy reaches the age of six months with floppy ears, taping may be necessary. Taping consists of elevating the ear and affixing it with tape. This, in effect, "trains" the ear to stand erect.

The ears of the Standard Manchester in the United States are cropped to a point. The cropping procedure only determines 50 percent of the resulting ear carriage, just as important is the aftercare your Manchester receives. Be sure that the person cropping your dog's ears is well aware of the specifics concerning the Manchester Terrier, as ear cropping is not the same for every breed. View pictures of champion Manchesters or contact a breeder with experience in cropping.

Finally, Manchester Terriers generally do not experience any trouble with the emergence of their permanent teeth. Some slight defects present in temporary teeth may correct with the arrival of permanent teeth. There is a tendency for the Toy Manchester Terrier to retain temporary teeth after the permanent teeth appear; in this case, extraction is recommended.

RECOGNIZED PROBLEMS

It is important to remember that a Manchester Terrier, either Standard or Toy, purchased from a reputable breeder should be carefully screened and therefore, will rarely be subject to congenital defects.

Skin Irritations

Any dog, no matter how well bred, may suffer a skin

Regular medical care is extremely important throughout your Manchester Terrier's life. Vaccination boosters and regular physical exams are part of your dog's lifelong maintenance.

irritation now and then. The Manchester Terrier is particularly prone to this type of difficulty, and skin irritations often become infections that may be incorrectly diagnosed as demodectic mange. These infections result in enflamed skin, sores, and hair loss. Regular grooming will help to combat irritations, as well as become part of the cure once an infection is contracted. A commercially prepared shampoo containing lanolin and formulated especially for dogs will be soothing, as well as promote hair growth and skin health. At the first sign of irritation, you should bring your Manchester Terrier to the veterinarian.

Grand Mal Epilepsy

Epilepsy is a cerebral disorder characterized by irregular convulsive seizures. It may be encountered at any age and is not so much a characteristic of the breed though it is evident in some family lines. In a grand mal seizure, there is a loss of consciousness and an involuntary contraction of all the muscles in the body, lasting for at least a few minutes. There are tests to diagnose the disorder and the severity of the infliction varies with each animal. Various courses of treatment are available—all with moderate success.

Secondary Glaucoma (Lens Luxation)

Secondary glaucoma is not an uncommon malady of the Manchester Terrier. Pressure builds inside the eyeball, pushing the lens outward of its normal alignment. This type of glaucoma does not respond to nonsurgical therapies, and eventually the lens must be removed.

Ehlers-Danlos Syndrome (Cutaneous Asthenia)

Literally a weakness of the skin, cutaneous asthenia can be found in male or female dogs. It is an inherited dominant trait that is always manifested; there is no such thing as a carrier of this condition. Symptoms include fragility of the skin, hyper—extensibility, and laxity. Lacerations are easily produced in dogs with this abnormality. The skin of animals that suffer from this have wide pliable scars and hematomas may develop at the site of injury. The skin has a moist blanched appearance and feels silky to the touch. Affected animals should not be bred.

Von Willebrand's Disease

An inherited disorder that causes the blood's clotting

factor to fail, von Willebrand's disease is found in some lines of Manchester Terrier, more so in the Toy than the Standard. The abnormal gene can be inherited from both parents; the result is often death. However, in most cases the extent of the disease varies from pup to pup. Percentage of the clotting factor will vary; one dog may have 15 percent of the clotting factor, another may have 60 percent. Obviously, the more clotting factor present, the less spontaneous bleeding will occur. There are tests on the market to determine the amount of von Willebrand factor in the blood and they are accurate and reasonably priced. Manchester Terriers who carry the disease should never be used for breeding.

Vaccination Reaction

Manchester Terriers have been known to suffer drastic reactions after immunization. Because of this, they are not only prone to upsets in growth and development, but also risk going into anaphylactic shock. This type of shock is a severe sensitivity to a foreign protein that has entered into the body. The symptoms and severity of the shock varies with the nervous system of the individual Manchester Terrier. If you observe signs of shock—vomiting, rapid pulse, diarrhea, and eventual physical collapse—keep the dog warm and get him to the veterinarian immediately. There are a variety of treatments to ease your dog out of shock. Untreated, a dog that is in a state of shock may die. Many breeders feel that because of this propensity, Manchester Terriers should be vaccinated with reduced doses, even if repeated doses are necessary.

Sensitivity to Anesthesia

Manchester Terriers have special needs in the event that they must be sedated with anesthesia. First, the veterinarian administering the anesthetic should not rely entirely on the weight-dosage ratio. It is extremely important that the vital signs of the dog are monitored at all times and the level of anesthetization is judged in accordance.

Secondly, prior to any procedure in which the animal must be anesthetized, the dog should be hydrated with a water solution administered subcutaneously. Be sure that your veterinarian is familiar with this problem before sedating your Manchester Terrier.

Finally, anesthetization can put strain on a Manchester Terrier's heart. Again, be sure that heart rate and pulse are monitored closely at all times.

YOUR HEALTHY MANCHESTER TERRIER

Dogs, like all other animals, are capable of contracting problems and diseases that, in most cases, are easily avoided by sound husbandry—meaning well-bred and well-cared-for animals are less prone to developing diseases and problems than are carelessly bred and neglected animals. Your knowledge of how to avoid problems is far more valuable than all of the books and advice on how to cure them. Respectively, the only person you should listen to about treatment is your vet. Veterinarians don't have all the answers, but at least they are trained to analyze and treat illnesses, and are aware of the full implications of treatments. This does not mean a few old remedies aren't good standbys when all else fails, but in most cases modern science provides the best treatments for disease.

Opposite: For the sake of your dog as well as the health of your family, you should bring your new Manchester Terrier to the veterinarian within three days of his arrival at your home.

PHYSICAL EXAMS

Your puppy should receive regular physical examinations or check-ups. These come in two forms. One is obviously performed by your vet, and the other is a day-to-day procedure that should be done by you. Apart from the fact the exam will highlight any problem at an early stage, it is an excellent way of socializing the pup to being handled.

To do the physical exam yourself, start at the head and work your way around the body. You are looking for any sign of lesions, or any indication of parasites on the pup. The most common parasites are fleas and ticks.

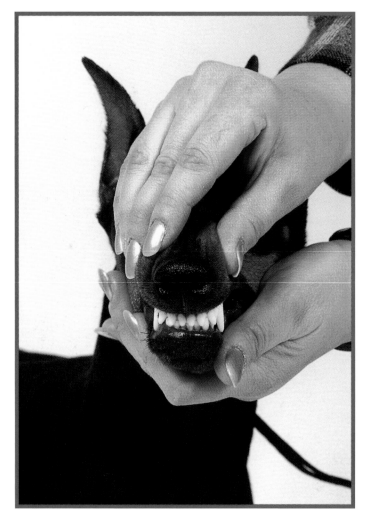

A thorough examination of your Manchester Terrier's mouth, teeth, and gums should be part of his annual checkup.

HEALTHY TEETH AND GUMS

Chewing is instinctual. Puppies chew so that their teeth and jaws grow strong and healthy as they develop. As the permanent teeth begin to emerge, it is painful and annoying to the puppy, and puppy owners must recognize that their new charges need something safe upon which to chew. Unfortunately, once the puppy's permanent teeth have emerged and settled solidly into the jaw, the chewing instinct does not fade. Adult dogs instinctively need to clean their teeth, massage their gums, and exercise their jaws through chewing.

It is necessary for your dog to have clean teeth. You should take your dog to the veterinarian at least once a year to have his teeth cleaned and to have his mouth examined for any sign of oral disease. Although dogs do not get cavities in the same way humans do, dogs'

The Hercules™ by Nylabone® has raised dental tips that help fight plaque on your Manchester Terrier's teeth and gums.

teeth accumulate tartar, and more quickly than humans do! Veterinarians recommend brushing your dog's teeth daily. But who can find time to brush their dog's teeth daily? The accumulation of tartar and plaque on our dog's teeth when not removed can cause irritation and eventually erode the enamel and finally destroy the teeth. Advanced cases, while destroying the teeth, bring on gingivitis and periodontitis, two very serious conditions that can affect the dog's internal organs as well...to say nothing about bad breath!

Raised dental tips on the surface of every Plaque Attacker™ help to combat plaque and tartar.

Since everyone can't brush their dog's teeth daily or get to the veterinarian often enough for him to scale

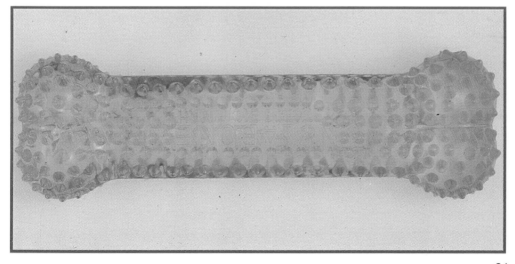

the dog's teeth, providing the dog with something safe to chew on will help maintain oral hygeine. Chew devices from Nylabone® keep dogs' teeth clean, but they also provide an excellent resource for entertainment and relief of doggie tensions. Nylabone® products give your dog something to do for an hour or two every day and during that hour or two, your dog will be taking an active part in keeping his teeth and gums healthy…without even realizing it! That's invaluable to your dog, and valuable to you!

Nylabone® provides fun bones, challenging bones, and *safe* bones. It is an owner's responsibility to recognize safe chew toys from dangerous ones. Your dog will chew and devour anything you give him. Dogs must not be permitted to chew on items that they can break. Pieces of broken objects can do internal damage to a dog, besides ripping the dog's mouth. Cheap plastic or rubber toys can cause stoppage in the intestines; such stoppages are operable only if caught immediately.

The most obvious choices, in this case, may be the worst choice. Natural beef bones were not designed for chewing and cannot take too much pressure from the sides. Due to the abrasive nature of these bones, they should be offered most sparingly. Knuckle bones, though once very popular for dogs, can be easily

Nylabone® is the only plastic dog bone made of 100 percent virgin nylon, specially processed to create a tough, durable, completely safe bone.

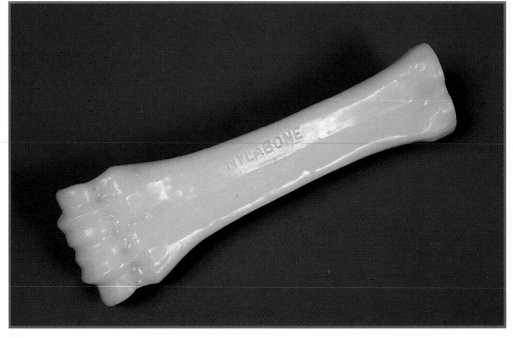

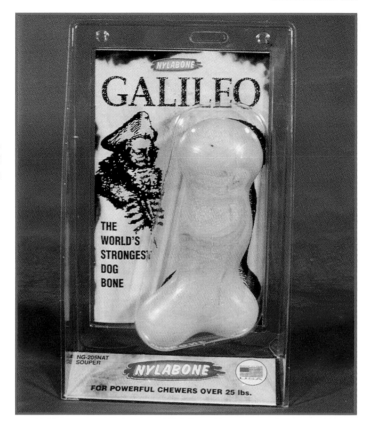

The Galileo™ is flavored to appeal to your dog and annealed so it has a relatively soft outer layer.

chewed up and eaten by dogs. At the very least, digestion is interrupted; at worst, the dog can choke or suffer from intestinal blockage.

When a dog chews hard on a Nylabone®, little bristle-like projections appear on the surface of the bone. These help to clean the dog's teeth and add to the gum-massaging. Given the chemistry of the nylon, the bristle can pass through the dog's intestinal tract without effect. Since nylon is inert, no microorganism can grow on it, and it can be washed in soap and water or sterilized in boiling water or in an autoclave.

For the sake of your dog, his teeth and your own peace of mind, provide your dog with Nylabones®. They have 100 variations from which to choose.

FIGHTING FLEAS

Fleas are very mobile and may be red, black, or brown in color. The adults suck the blood of the host, while the larvae feed on the feces of the adults, which is rich in blood. Flea "dirt" may be seen on the pup as very tiny clusters of blackish specks that look like freshly ground pepper. The eggs of fleas may be laid on the puppy, though they are more commonly laid off the host in a favorable place, such as the bedding. They normally hatch in 4 to 21 days, depending on the temperature, but they can survive for up to 18 months if temperature conditions are not favorable. The larvae are maggot-like and molt a couple of times before forming pupae, which can survive long periods until the temperature, or the vibration of a nearby host, causes them to emerge and jump on a host.

There are a number of effective treatments available, and you should discuss them with your veterinarian, then follow all instructions for the one you choose. Any treatment will involve a product for your puppy or dog and one for the environment, and will require diligence on your part to treat all areas and thoroughly clean your home and yard until the infestation is eradicated.

THE TROUBLE WITH TICKS

Ticks are arthropods of the spider family, which means they have eight legs (though the larvae have six). They bury their headparts into the host and gorge on its blood. They are easily seen as small grain-like creatures sticking out from the skin. They are often picked up when dogs play in fields, but may also arrive in your yard via wild animals—even birds—or stray cats and dogs. Some ticks are species-specific, others are more adaptable and will host on many species.

The cat flea is the most common flea of dogs. It starts feeding soon after it makes contact with the dog.

The deer tick is the most common carrier of Lyme disease. Photo courtesy of Virbac Laboratories, Inc., Fort Worth, Texas.

The most troublesome type of tick is the deer tick, which spreads the deadly Lyme disease that can cripple a dog (or a person). Deer ticks are tiny and very hard to detect. Often, by the time they're big enough to notice, they've been feeding on the dog for a few days—long enough to do their damage. Lyme disease was named for the area of the United States in which it was first detected—Lyme, Connecticut—but has now been diagnosed in almost all parts of the U.S. Your veterinarian can advise you of the danger to your dog(s) in your area, and may suggest your dog be vaccinated for Lyme. Always go over your dog with a fine-toothed flea comb when you come in from walking through any area that may harbor deer ticks, and if your dog is acting unusually sluggish or sore, seek veterinary advice.

Attempts to pull a tick free will invariably leave the headpart in the pup, where it will die and cause an infected wound or abscess. The best way to remove ticks is to dab a strong saline solution, iodine, or alcohol on them. This will numb them, causing them to loosen their hold, at which time they can be removed with forceps. The wound can then be cleaned and covered with an antiseptic ointment. If ticks are common in your area, consult with your vet for a suitable pesticide to be used in kennels, on bedding, and on the puppy or dog.

INSECTS AND OTHER OUTDOOR DANGERS

There are many biting insects, such as mosquitoes, that can cause discomfort to a puppy. Many diseases are transmitted by the males of these species.

A pup can easily get a grass seed, fox tail, or thorn lodged between his pads or in the folds of his ears. These may go unnoticed until an abscess forms.

This is where your daily check of the puppy or dog will do a world of good. If your puppy has been playing in long grass or places where there may be thorns, pine needles, wild animals, or parasites, the check-up is a wise precaution.

Your Manchester Terriers should be energetic and alert. Any changes in their activity should be brought to your veterinarian's attention immediately.

SKIN DISORDERS

Apart from problems associated with lesions created by biting pests, a puppy may fall foul to a number of other skin disorders. Examples are ringworm, mange, and eczema. Ringworm is not caused by a worm, but is a fungal infection. It manifests itself as a sore-looking bald circle. If your puppy should have any form of bald patches, let your veterinarian check him over; a microscopic examination can confirm the condition. Many old remedies for ringworm exist, such as iodine, carbolic acid, formalin, and other tinctures, but modern drugs are superior.

Fungal infections can be very difficult to treat, and even more difficult to eradicate, because of the spores. These can withstand most treatments, other than burning, which is the best thing to do with bedding once the condition has been confirmed.

Mange is a general term that can be applied to many skin conditions where the hair falls out and a flaky crust develops and falls away.

Often, dogs will scratch themselves, and this invariably is worse than the original condition, for it opens lesions that are then subject to viral, fungal, or parasitic attack. The cause of the problem can be various species of mites. These either live on skin debris and the hair follicles, which they destroy, or they bury themselves just beneath the skin and feed on the tissue. Applying general remedies from pet stores is not recommended because it is essential to identify the type of mange before a specific treatment is effective.

Eczema is another non-specific term applied to many skin disorders. The condition can be brought about in many ways. Sunburn, chemicals, allergies to foods, drugs, pollens, and even stress can all produce a deterioration of the skin and coat. Given the range of causal factors, treatment can be difficult because the problem is one of identification. It is a case of taking each possibility at a time and trying to correctly diagnose the matter. If the cause is of a dietary nature then you must remove one item at a time in order to find out if the dog is allergic to a given food. It could, of course, be the lack of a nutrient that is the problem, so if the condition persists, you should consult your veterinarian.

INTERNAL DISORDERS

It cannot be overstressed that it is very foolish to attempt to diagnose an internal disorder without the advice of a veterinarian. Take a relatively common problem such as diarrhea. It might be caused by nothing more serious than the puppy hogging a lot of food or eating something that it has never previously eaten. Conversely, it could be the first indication of a potentially fatal disease. It's up to your veterinarian to make the correct diagnosis.

The following symptoms, especially if they accompany each other or are progressively added to earlier symptoms, mean you should visit the veterinarian right away:

Continual vomiting. All dogs vomit from time to time and this is not necessarily a sign of illness. They will eat grass to induce vomiting. It is a natural cleansing process common to many carnivores. However, continued vomiting is a clear sign of a problem. It may be a blockage in the pup's intestinal tract, it may be induced by worms, or it could be due to any number of diseases.

Diarrhea. This, too, may be nothing more than a temporary condition due to many factors. Even a change of home can induce diarrhea, because this often stresses the pup, and invariably there is some change in the diet. If it persists more than 48 hours then something is amiss. If blood is seen in the feces, waste no time at all in taking the dog to the vet.

Running eyes and/or nose. A pup might have a chill and this will cause the eyes and nose to weep. Again, this should quickly clear up if the puppy is placed in a warm environment and away from any drafts. If it does not, and especially if a mucous discharge is seen, then the pup has an illness that must be diagnosed.

Coughing. Prolonged coughing is a sign of a problem, usually of a respiratory nature.

Wheezing. If the pup has difficulty breathing and makes a wheezing sound when breathing, then something is wrong.

Cries when attempting to defecate or urinate. This might only be a minor problem due to the hard state of the feces, but it could be more serious, especially if the pup cries when urinating.

Cries when touched. Obviously, if you do not handle a puppy with care he might yelp. However, if he cries even when lifted gently, then he has an internal problem that becomes apparent when pressure is applied to a given area of the body. Clearly, this must be diagnosed.

Refuses food. Generally, puppies and dogs are greedy creatures when it comes to feeding time. Some might be more fussy, but none should refuse more than one meal. If they go for a number of hours without showing any interest in their food, then something is not as it should be.

General listlessness. All puppies have their off days when they do not seem their usual cheeky, mischievous selves. If this condition persists for more than two days then there is little doubt of a problem. They may not show any of the signs listed, other than perhaps a reduced interest in their food. There are many diseases that can develop internally without displaying obvious clinical signs. Blood, fecal, and other tests are needed in order to identify the disorder before it reaches an advanced state that may not be treatable.

WORMS

There are many species of worms, and a number of these live in the tissues of dogs and most other animals. Many create no problem at all, so you are not even aware they exist. Others can be tolerated in small levels, but become a major problem if they number more than a few. The most common types seen in dogs are roundworms and tapeworms. While roundworms are the greater problem, tapeworms require an intermediate host so are more easily eradicated.

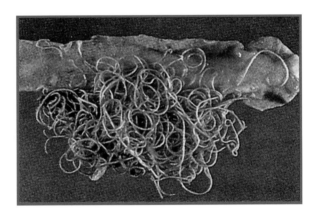

Roundworms are spaghetti-like worms that cause a pot-bellied appearance and dull coat, along with more severe symptoms, such as diarrhea and vomiting. Photo courtesy of Merck AgVet.

Roundworms of the species *Toxocara canis* infest the dog. They may grow to a length of 8 inches (20 cm) and look like strings of spaghetti. The worms feed on the digesting food in the pup's intestines. In chronic cases the puppy will become pot-bellied, have diarrhea, and will vomit. Eventually, he will stop eating, having passed through the stage when he always seems hungry. The worms lay eggs in the puppy and these pass out in his feces. They are then either ingested by the pup, or they are eaten by mice, rats, or beetles. These may then be eaten by the puppy and the life cycle is complete.

Larval worms can migrate to the womb of a pregnant bitch, or to her mammary glands, and this is how they pass to the puppy. The pregnant bitch can be wormed, which will help. The pups can, and should,

Whipworms are hard to find unless you strain your dog's feces, and this is best left to a veterinarian. Pictured here are adult whipworms.

be wormed when they are about two weeks old. Repeat worming every 10 to 14 days and the parasites should be removed. Worms can be extremely dangerous to young puppies, so you should be sure the pup is wormed as a matter of routine.

Tapeworms can be seen as tiny rice-like eggs sticking to the puppy's or dog's anus. They are less destructive, but still undesirable. The eggs are eaten by mice, fleas, rabbits, and other animals that serve as intermediate hosts. They develop into a larval stage and the host must be eaten by the dog in order to complete the chain. Your vet will supply a suitable remedy if tapeworms are seen or suspected. There are other worms, such as hookworms and whipworms, that are also blood suckers. They will make a pup anemic, and blood might be seen in the feces, which can be examined by the vet to confirm their presence. Cleanliness in all matters is the best preventative measure for all worms.

Heartworm infestation in dogs is passed by mosquitoes but can be prevented by a monthly (or daily) treatment that is given orally. Talk to your vet about the risk of heartworm in your area.

BLOAT (GASTRIC DILATATION)

This condition has proved fatal in many dogs, especially large and deep-chested breeds, such as the Weimaraner and the Great Dane. However, any dog can get bloat. It is caused by swallowing air during exercise, food/water gulping or another strenuous task. As many believe, it is not the result of flatulence. The stomach of an affected dog twists, disallowing food and blood flow and resulting in harmful toxins being released into the bloodstream. Death can easily follow if the condition goes undetected.

The best preventative measure is not to feed large meals or exercise your puppy or dog immediately after he has eaten. Veterinarians recommend feeding three smaller meals per day in an elevated feeding rack, adding water to dry food to prevent gulping, and not offering water during mealtimes.

VACCINATIONS

Every puppy, purebred or mixed breed, should be vaccinated against the major canine diseases. These are distemper, leptospirosis, hepatitis, and canine parvovirus. Your puppy may have received a temporary vaccination against distemper before you purchased him, but be sure to ask the breeder to be sure.

The age at which vaccinations are given can vary, but will usually be when the pup is 8 to 12 weeks old. By this time any protection given to the pup by antibodies received from his mother via her initial milk feeds will be losing their strength.

Rely on your veterinarian for the most effectual vaccination schedule for your Manchester Terrier puppy.

The puppy's immune system works on the basis that the white blood cells engulf and render harmless

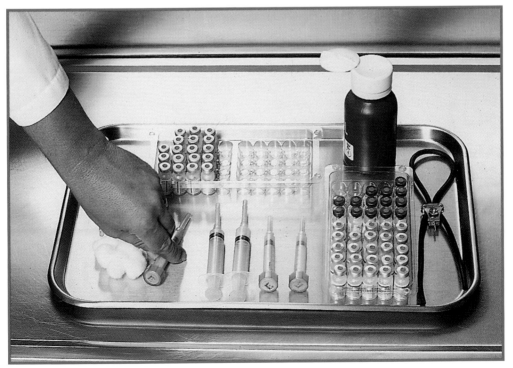

attacking bacteria. However, they must first recognize a potential enemy.

Vaccines are either dead bacteria or they are live, but in very small doses. Either type prompts the pup's defense system to attack them. When a large attack then comes (if it does), the immune system recognizes it and massive numbers of lymphocytes (white blood corpuscles) are mobilized to counter the attack. However, the ability of the cells to recognize these dangerous viruses can diminish over a period of time. It is therefore useful to provide annual reminders about the nature of the enemy. This is done by means of booster injections that keep the immune system on its alert. Immunization is not 100-percent guaranteed to be successful, but is very close. Certainly it is better than giving the puppy no protection.

Dogs are subject to other viral attacks, and if these are of a high-risk factor in your area, then your vet will suggest you have the puppy vaccinated against these as well.

Your puppy or dog should also be vaccinated against the deadly rabies virus. In fact, in many places it is illegal for your dog not to be vaccinated. This is to protect your dog, your family, and the rest of the animal population from this deadly virus that infects the nervous system and causes dementia and death.

ACCIDENTS

All puppies will get their share of bumps and bruises due to the rather energetic way they play. These will usually heal themselves over a few days. Small cuts should be bathed with a suitable disinfectant and then smeared with an antiseptic ointment. If a cut looks more serious, then stem the flow of blood with a towel or makeshift tourniquet and rush the pup to the veterinarian. Never apply so much pressure to the wound that it might restrict the flow of blood to the limb.

In the case of burns you should apply cold water or an ice pack to the surface. If the burn was due to a chemical, then this must be washed away with copious amounts of water. Apply petroleum jelly, or any vegetable oil, to the burn. Trim away the hair if need be. Wrap the dog in a blanket and rush him to the vet. The pup may go into shock, depending on the severity of the burn, and this will result in a lowered blood pressure, which is dangerous and the reason the pup must receive immediate veterinary attention.